ASHLEY JUDICE

Sensory Mindfulness

30 Ways to Calm Overstimulation and Cultivate Inner Balance

First edition

This book was professionally typeset on Reedsy.
Find out more at reedsy.com

Contents

1 Introduction   1

2 The Visual Realm   3

Develop Visual Awareness   4

Build an Aesthetically Pleasing Environment   5

Cultivate Mindful Art Appreciation   6

3 The Auditory Realm   8

Mindful Sound Meditation   9

Create Soothing Soundscapes   10

Mindful Communication and Active Listening   10

4 The Tactile Realm   12

Mindful Body Scan & Progressive Muscle Relaxation   13

Exploring Platonic Touch   14

Engaging with Textures and Sensory Materials   14

5 The Olfactory Realm   16

Aromatherapy and Essential Oils   17

Mindful Cooking and Flavor Appreciation   18

6 The Gustatory Realm   19

Bring Awareness to the Act of Eating   20

Cultivating a Mindful Relationship with Food   20

Mindful Eating for Emotional Balance   21

7 Conclusion   22

8 References   24

1

Introduction

With today's technological advancements, we are the only generation with access to vast amounts of information at our fingertips. Literally. To say that it can become overwhelming and distracting would be an understatement. We have access to local and national news, global news, and many conflicting opinions on each situation. In addition to that input, we live our own lives with physical and mental struggles. Sometimes, we need to take a minute to breathe.

Close your eyes and breathe in deeply. Clear your mind as you breathe out the tension you are holding. Breathe in again, and hold it for the count of four. Let it out.

That was a mindful moment. It was being present in your body and disengaging from negative thoughts. It seems simple enough, but it isn't easy. Staying present in the moment takes practice. We can easily fall into negative loops, which are negative thoughts that lead to other negative thoughts, and we need to break the cycle of thinking. Sometimes the best way to get out of your head space is to use your physical senses to break the mental loop. This is called sensory mindfulness.

Several studies have linked mindful practices with stress management, anxiety reduction, and other health benefits. One study found measurable improvement in memory, learning, and emotion, while another found reduced anxiety and hostility (Wein, 2012). In general, those with routine mindfulness practices tend to feel more competent, self-sufficient and have more positive relationships.

The goal of mindfulness is not to avoid or ignore negative thoughts but to acknowledge and release them. Many things are out of your control, such as other people's reactions to events or external stimuli. Mindfulness can clear your anxiety and allow you to focus on the things you control and choose an action to take. Remember, a blank mind is not the goal; bringing focus to the present moment is.

As humans, we experience life in multisensory environments. This means that we constantly receive stimuli from all of our senses. With that in mind, we will focus on how the five senses can help bring awareness to your present physical state for mental clarity. When you start your mindful practice, it is recommended to begin with your learning preference. So, visual learners may want to start practicing visual mindfulness; aural learners may wish to begin with auditory mindfulness; kinetic learners may want to start with tactile mindfulness. However you choose to begin, ensure the techniques resonate with you, are practical to implement in your daily routine, and can be accessed from wherever you are.

2

The Visual Realm

For many people, vision is used to find something attractive to consume or possess. People spend countless hours watching or re-watching movies and shows. Pictures used in menus help diners choose their next meal. Vision boards can help people achieve their goals by allowing them to see an outcome. Sensory mindfulness uses vision to slow or stop a negative thought loop.

"It seems to me that the natural world is the greatest source of excitement; the greatest source of visual beauty; the greatest source of intellectual interest. It is the greatest source of so much in life that makes life worth living." - David Attenborough

Develop Visual Awareness

Mindful observation is one way that you can develop your visual awareness. Choose an object that is near you to focus on. Take in the object's distinctive colors, shape, and size. Then start to take note of the more minor things; are the edges worn, is there something missing or out of place, are there fine details you have not noticed before? Depending on your surroundings, you may want to set a timer to return to your previous task with a clear mind.

Mindful gazing meditation is another way to strengthen your visual awareness. This technique may also be a tool for practicing short-term memory recall. Choose a spot to sit; if on the ground, get into your preferred meditation posture; if in a chair, plant both feet on the ground, sit straight up, and rest your hands on your lap or the armrests. Choose an object and gaze at a fixed central point. When your eyes become tired, close them and notice the "afterimage" in your mind. Open your eyes and repeat the process when you can no longer focus.

There are variations of gazing meditation that you may want to explore. "Trataka," or candle gazing, has been practiced since the 15th century in India (Mayer, 2022). Find your position in a dark room, set a one-minute timer, and gaze at a lit candle. Follow the flow of the flame with your eyes; try not to blink often. When your eyes tire, close them and find the flame's "afterimage" in your mind. If you are a beginner, you should only practice this for three to five minutes, then work toward longer sessions (Mayer, 2022).

Mirror gazing meditation is another variation to try. Find your position in front of a mirror, preferably seated, set your timer for five minutes, and gaze into your own eyes. This can initially feel uncomfortable, but the practice may boost your self-compassion, authenticity, and emotional awareness (Raypole, 2020). During your observation, you may notice the areas where you carry tension or see the emotion in how you hold yourself. Notice and release the thought. If you are carrying tension, consider incorporating some tactile mindfulness into your practice to deepen your self-awareness.

Build an Aesthetically Pleasing Environment

You have a right to feel comfortable in a space that you frequent. This can be your home, your office, or even your vehicle. Build an environment in which you feel peaceful and calm. One way that you can try is the Feng Shui method. Feng Shui encompasses several principles, including yin and yang energies, the five natural elements, the Bagua Map, colors, commanding position, and mirrors (Migala et al., 2023). Each of these has many ways to implement in any space. Adding a few elements can improve your perception of the area and how you use it. Research and find which principles resonate the most with you and the space you are enhancing.

Another way to elevate your space is to incorporate nature-inspired elements into your decor. If you prefer the neutral browns and oranges of the desert, paint an accent wall or add throw pillows to your seating areas. You could even add a shag carpet in these tones to make space for tactile mindfulness practices. There is no limit to your creativity!

Some have found that removing items from their space can bring about peace. A "minimalist living" movement has recently liberated many from material objects. This alone may release visual overstimulation and promote a calm environment. Eliminating distractions is at the core of mindfulness; finding a distraction-free space can be a big step toward inner balance. If you live with other people, it may be that the only area you can clear is your vehicle or your room. If you are transforming your office or cubicle, try putting everything in a box and only bringing out those things that serve the emotion you want to amplify. If you want to transition toward minimalism but are not ready to overhaul your space, try doing one small piece at a time. Clear the bedside table today, and maybe in a couple of days, clear the dresser top. Remember that you are nurturing yourself through your environment. If you must work slowly and gently, then do so.

Cultivate Mindful Art Appreciation

With all of the visual stimulation that we have access to through our screens, it can be easy to forget that there are museums that hold physical art. Take a day and visit a museum or art gallery. Observe a piece at different distances, at different angles. Focus on the experience of it all. Read the piece's title and imagine how the artist determined the name. Furthermore, turn off your phone; view the art with your eyes, not through your phone lens.

Explore different art forms. Visual mindfulness is not limited to finished art. There are events and spaces where artisans practice historic trades such as blacksmithing and glassblowing for audiences to observe—watching a piece of art form before your eyes can help you be present in the work of another. You can follow the emotional impact of joy and pride when the piece is finished. You can also observe others in the space, whether an audience member's experience or a mentor guiding the artist, to watch their reactions to the process.

If the inspiration strikes you, create art as a meditative practice. Watching paint pulled slowly across the canvas by your own hand can increase your focus and help you feel a sense of control when you feel like you have none.

If you want a more profound experience, pair visual mindfulness techniques with other sensory realms. Pairing may not increase your focus on a particular action or stimulus, but it may help you savor the moment and get some dopamine to pause that negative loop.

3

The Auditory Realm

There is a lot of commotion in the world today. It can be so overwhelming that it has been called noise pollution. With the introduction of devices that offer noise cancellation or transparent hearing options, we can literally "turn down" the volume of the world around us. On the other hand, we can turn up the subwoofers and get lost in the music. Sound can be both filling and draining; notice how different sounds make you feel. Cultivate those that help bring you into the present and relax you.

"People say that the Soul, on hearing the song of creation, entered the body, but in reality, the Soul itself was the Song." – Hafiz (1320-1390)

Mindful Sound Meditation

Some people prefer to meditate in silence to focus on sorting through their thoughts and releasing negativity. Others prefer to meditate with noise present to clear their mind of negativity before sorting their thoughts. Sound meditation is a practice that focuses on the sounds you can hear. Choose a spot with the level of noise you prefer, set your timer, and find your position. This can be sitting on a blanket on a park green, at home with a playlist of nature sounds, or on a bench at the mall. Close your eyes, or hold a soft gaze at a fixed position, and turn your attention to the sounds you can hear. Try to pick out individual layers of the soundscape. Can you tell whether someone is approaching or passing you by the direction and volume of their voice? Try to expand your awareness to subtler sounds. Can you find the sound of the wind under the songs of the birds? Remember to listen and let go. Don't narrate the surroundings; observe.

A variation of sound meditation uses music rather than natural or environmental sounds. Some prefer classical music to sit and focus on; some prefer measured bass lines, and others prefer quick guitar riffs. Start with your favorite music genre and find a groove that works for you. If you are ready to move to another genre, but don't know which one to try, research your favorite artist's inspiration. You may be pleasantly surprised at similarities across genres.

A different type of sound meditation uses tones and vibrations to help support deep relaxation. Some people prefer a singing bowl's tones, while others prefer specific hertz frequencies. There are many options; half the fun is discovering new sounds and feeling them resonate within you.

Create Soothing Soundscapes

Research has shown that people are influenced by sound in their environment and vice versa, that people influence sound around them. This means that our daily noise exposure can mentally and physically affect us (Chen & Ma, 2020). Competing sounds can cause overstimulation. Curating personal playlists is an intentional way to create a sound environment that can evoke calm and bring you to a peaceful place wherever you are. Don't limit yourself to just one playlist. Just as certain types or beats of music can make an energizing workout or cleaning playlist, other types can make a productive study session or pleasant dining experience.

Design your acoustic environments for relaxation and focus. Studies on pleasant soundscapes have found an association between a "faster stress-recovery process and better self-reported health condition" (Chen & Ma, 2020). It has become so important that laws and regulations have been enacted to mitigate noise levels in several countries. If you don't live in an area with quality acoustic environments, you can adjust your space yourself or hire a professional. Noise reduction is possible with wall soundproofing with acoustic panels, door soundproofing by filling air gaps around the edges, or floor soundproofing with carpet or rugs.

Mindful Communication and Active Listening

With all the sounds available to us at any given time, we can sometimes overlook the need to hear another person's voice. The sound of someone's voice can bring back memories; their tone and intention can bring relief and peace. While communication may not seem significant when considering sensory mindfulness, it is a way to be intentional and present in our social relationships.

Loneliness is a perceived social isolation, not necessarily an accurate measure of social interactions and relationships (Masi et al., 2011). Feeling as though no one listens or understands you can create barriers to communication that could help relieve stress and tension. Active listening is one of the best ways to cultivate trusted relationships with others. Ways to show active listening during a conversation are focusing on what the speaker is saying, having no distractions, and engaging the dialogue with questions and encouraging responses. Practicing simple conversations with active listening builds good habits to fall back on when you need deeper conversations. When you have people you are comfortable speaking with regarding overwhelming and negative feelings, calling or texting is a great way to work through the negative loop.

By cultivating mindful listening skills and attuning to the auditory realm, we enhance our ability to appreciate and engage with sound and contribute to our overall sensory balance. Auditory mindfulness serves as a gateway to a deeper sensory awareness, laying the foundation for a more profound and integrated experience of sensory mindfulness.

4

The Tactile Realm

Sometimes we move so fast that only physical pain will slow us down. Our bodies hold tension when we are mentally stressed. Shoulders creep up towards our ears. Jaws clench. And most of the time, we are unaware that we are doing it. Tactile awareness and mindfulness are pivotal in our overall sensory balance, anchoring us in the present moment and connecting us to our physical selves. There is such a strong connection between body and mind that you should incorporate corporeal awareness, touch, and texture into your mindful practice or daily routine.

"Take care of your body. It's the only place you have to live." - Jim Rohn

Mindful Body Scan & Progressive Muscle Relaxation

A body scan is a meditation that focuses on bodily awareness of sensations felt physically. Studies have shown that those who practice body scan meditation can experience improved sleep, anxiety and stress relief, greater self-awareness and self-compassion, and reduced pain (Raypole, 2022). Choose a spot and find your position, preferably where you can stretch or move easily. Begin by centering your awareness on your breath. Choose where on your body you want to start, like the top of your head, and focus on that particular spot. Pay attention to and acknowledge any discomfort, pain, or tension. After 30 seconds, move on to the next part of your body with complete focus. Continue in this manner until the whole body has been scanned. If you feel your mind wandering from the task, gently bring your thoughts back to the breath and the physical sensations. If this is new to you, many guided meditations are available to help keep you on track with your focus.

Progressive muscle relaxation is a variation of the body scan practice. When in position, begin focusing on your feet. Squeeze those muscles, curl your toes, count to five, and release. Repeat twice more in the same area before moving to the next part of your body. Move either up or down your body as you see fit. The idea is to train your body to relax when you need to slow your physical stress response (Deuster, 2022).

Exploring Platonic Touch

As individuals working long hours and living our lives, sometimes we forget how important touch can be. Studies show that holding hands, hugging, or cuddling can lower blood pressure, reduce stress, and increase immunity (Leavitt, 2022). Combining the platonic touch with active listening skills can further strengthen social bonds with others. While it may seem out of reach for some, consider that close relationships like friends and family can offer hugs, hold hands across a table, or any other meaningful platonic touch. For those in romantic relationships, consider that not every physical contact has to be sexual - when was the last time you held hands intending to feel closer to each other? Strengthening a friendship within a romantic relationship can build a foundation for support in calming overstimulation in daily life.

Another place to find peace is in the companionship of a pet. While dogs, cats, and other furred creatures may be soft to pet, some prefer the feeling of holding snakes or other reptiles. If pet ownership is not an option for your living situation or work-life balance, consider visiting friends or family with pets or volunteering at a local animal shelter.

Engaging with Textures and Sensory Materials

Touching textures in our environment is one way to bring you into the moment. When you handle an object, focus on feeling the shape, roughness, or smoothness rather than seeing it - close your eyes for a different experience. If you can step outdoors, take a moment to breathe in the fresh air and feel the material you are leaning against or seated on. Concrete, wood, or steel benches have interesting textures, especially when they are a little worn. Kinetic sand is a great way to get the unique feeling of sand without the mess or the drive to the beach. Another exciting texture is dry rice or beans in a bag; transfer them into a storage bag or plastic container and immerse your hand in them. The world around us contains interesting things; let your curiosity guide you.

By embracing tactile awareness and practicing mindfulness in our physical encounters, we unlock the harmonious integration of all our senses. Remember that feeling comfortable touching others in a consenting and platonic way may take some time to settle into. Be sure to give yourself grace as you incorporate physicality into your daily practice.

5

The Olfactory Realm

Have you ever caught a whiff of something and been immediately transported through time and space to a memory? That is the power of the olfactory system, your sense of smell. Scents and odors are sent to the limbic system of our brains, where emotions are processed and memory formation happens (Bentley et al., 2022). By exploring mindful aromatherapy, flavor appreciation, and creating soothing scent environments, we will unlock the transformative potential of olfactory mindfulness in our pursuit of inner balance.

"Smell the roses. Smell the coffee. Whatever it is that makes you happy." - Rita Moreno

Aromatherapy and Essential Oils

There has been a recent interest in using aromatherapy for self-healing, and there is more recognition of its benefits in the medical field. Aromatherapy uses the distilled extracts of plants to promote health. Many ancient cultures have rituals surrounding the use of aromatic plants and botanicals for medicine or religious purposes (Cronkleton, 2019). Today oils, balms, bathing salts, candles, and diffusers are readily available for you to incorporate into your space or on your body. Research has shown that aromatherapy can improve sleep quality, reduce stress, agitation, and anxiety, treat headaches and migraines, and even fight bacteria (Cronkleton, 2019).

A word of caution, do not apply essential oils directly to your skin; use a carrier oil. Do your research on applying oils and lotions to your skin, and work with your care provider if you have pre-existing conditions that may be negatively exacerbated by application. If you want to wear the scent but prefer not to have it on your skin, you can wear accessories such as necklaces and bracelets designed to hold the fragrance.

To amplify the impact of aromatherapy, create personalized scent pro-files for different purposes. Different scents like lavender, chamomile, and bergamot can promote a calming environment. Citrus scents can bring a refreshing element to your space and give you a little energy boost. Having several to choose from can change your environment without changing your area.

Sometimes you may not have quick access to an aroma that can calm you. Try taking a break near a particularly fragrant area. Coffee shops have beautiful scents you can get lost in; volunteer to do a coffee run and revel in the smell of ground coffee beans while waiting in line.

Mindful Cooking and Flavor Appreciation

For distinction, cooking and flavor appreciation are entirely separate from eating the final food product. Before eating, odors can orient and trigger our appetite (Boesveldt & Parma, 2021). The aromas during each step of the cooking process can bring your awareness to cooking and focus on your movements. Mindful cooking is slowing down the rush to get dinner on the table and enjoying the process. Carefully shop for fresh ingredients, evaluating and selecting each item by smell, touch, and sight. Each element in a recipe adds to the final flavor combination; slow down and observe their individual attributes. Preparing meals for others in this manner can bring about a sense of accomplishment and pride, contributing to feelings of self-worth, inner balance, and stronger social connections.

Our olfactory awareness seamlessly connects with the practice of gustatory mindfulness. Just as our sense of smell enhances our food experience, the flavors we savor also have the power to ignite memories and evoke emotions.

6

The Gustatory Realm

Personal relationships with food can be very complex. Some people find solace in comfort foods that remind them of home and feeling safe. Some people associate certain foods with accomplishments or as a reward. Others may find negative emotions or physical reactions when eating certain types of food. Our goal is to nurture a balanced relationship with food by enhancing our gustatory, or taste, awareness; to practice mindful eating for savoring the present moment.

"The appetite is sharpened by the first bites." - Jose Rizal (1861-1896)

Bring Awareness to the Act of Eating

Rushed meals can leave you feeling overstimulated and add stress to your day. Develop a practice of slow and mindful eating to enhance your taste appreciation. Take one bite at a time, chewing slowly. Pay attention to textures, flavors, and the entire sensory experience. Try closing your eyes to help focus on the release of flavors.

When dining out, many restaurants over-serve the customer. Keep overeating from ruining the experience by boxing up half your meal beforehand. Be sure to tune in to your hunger and fullness cues. Those last few bites may seem satisfying as you're chewing, but the discomfort afterward isn't worth it.

Cultivating a Mindful Relationship with Food

There are a lot of differing opinions about how people should and shouldn't consume food. These schools of thought may align with health or fitness goals, but all of this information and input can lead to overwhelm and confusion regarding your relationship with food.

One way to attain clarity is to develop a non-judgmental attitude toward food choices. Consider exploring the origins and stories behind ingredients and meals. Understanding and embracing the culture that brought the recipe into your kitchen can inspire further exploration and an appreciation for so much more. As discussed previously, engaging in mindful meal planning and preparation may contribute to a positive experience and long-term appreciation for food in general.

Mindful Eating for Emotional Balance

When people think about emotions concerning eating, there are immediately negative connotations put on the concept. Let's shift this mindset toward eating for emotional balance. Mindful eating uses all your physical and emotional senses to fully experience and enjoy your food choices (Cheung, 2023). Appreciate how the food looks, smells, and tastes. Consider how much work went into the making of the dish. Focusing on the present meal can increase feelings of gratitude, nourishment, pleasure, and satisfaction.

Mindful eating invites us to savor the present moment and cultivate a balanced relationship with food. It also contributes to sensory mindfulness and allows it to extend its reach into all aspects of our lives. It reminds us to engage fully with the world, appreciating the intricate tapestry of sensory experiences that shape our existence.

7

Conclusion

S
ensory mindfulness has been a journey of self-discovery, a path toward finding inner balance amidst the chaos of our sensory-rich world. We've explored the depths of visual observation, the symphony of sounds, the power of touch, evocative scents, and the flavors that ignite our taste buds. We've delved into sensory mindfulness through each chapter, equipping ourselves with practical tools and transformative insights.

Now, it's time for you to take these techniques and weave them into the fabric of your own life. Embrace the power of sensory mindfulness as a daily practice, allowing it to guide you toward a calmer, more harmonious existence. Pause and truly see the world around you, listen to the melodies of life, savor the textures and sensations, inhale deeply the scents that whisper stories, and taste each morsel with gratitude and presence.

But our journey does not end here. Your voice can inspire others on their path to inner balance. So, share your experience by leaving a heartfelt review of Sensory Mindfulness. Let others know how this book has transformed your perspective, awakened your senses, and enriched your life.

By sharing your thoughts, you become an advocate for the transformative potential of sensory mindfulness, igniting a ripple effect that extends far beyond the words on these pages. Let's create a community of mindful explorers united by our commitment to inner balance and sensory harmony. Your words have the power to shape and inspire, so take a moment to leave a review, and let us continue this journey of sensory mindfulness together.

May your senses remain in harmony, and may the path of sensory mindfulness lead you to a life of profound serenity and joy.

8

References

Bentley, P. R., Fisher, J. C., Dallimer, M., Fish, R. D., Austen, G. E., Irvine, K. N., & Davies, Z. G. (2022, July 18). *Nature, smells, and human wellbeing.* Ambio. https://www.ncbi.nlm.nih.gov/pmc/articles/PMC9289359/

Boesveldt, S., & Parma, V. (2021, January 12). *The importance of the olfactory system in human well-being, through nutrition and Social Behavior.* Cell and tissue research. https://www.ncbi.nlm.nih.gov/pmc/articles/PMC7802608/

Chen, J., & Ma, H. (2020, October 29). *A conceptual model of the Healthy Acoustic Environment: Elements, framework, and definition.* Frontiers in psychology. https://www.ncbi.nlm.nih.gov/pmc/articles/PMC7658336/

Cheung, L. (Ed.). (2023, February 2). *Mindful eating.* The Nutrition Source. https://www.hsph.harvard.edu/nutritionsource/mindful-eating/

Cronkleton, E. (2019, March 8). *What is aromatherapy and how does it help me?*. Healthline. https://www.healthline.com/health/what-is-aro matherapy#benefits

Deuster, P. (Ed.). (2022, May 9). *Everything you need to know about progressive muscle relaxation to boost your well-being and optimize performance.* HPRC. https://www.hprc-online.org/social-fitness/family-optimizati on/everything-you-need-know-about-progressive-muscle-relaxation

Leavitt, C. (2022, July 15). *Why non-sexual touch is so essential.* Psychology Today. https://www.psychologytoday.com/us/blog/sexual-mindf ulness/202207/why-non-sexual-touch-is-so-essential

Masi, C. M., Chen, H.-Y., Hawkley, L. C., & Cacioppo, J. T. (2011, August 17). *A meta-analysis of interventions to reduce loneliness.* Personality and social psychology review: an official journal of the Society for Personality and Social Psychology, Inc. https://www.ncbi.nlm.nih.gov/ pmc/articles/PMC3865701/

Mayer, B. A. (2022, January 11). *Can gazing at a candle flame increase your focus?*. Healthline. https://www.healthline.com/health/candle-me ditation

Migala, J., Cherney, K., Majsiak, B., Rapaport, L., Bedosky, L., Larson, J., Haupt, A., Louie, K., & Kovac, S. (2023, March 1). *What is Feng Shui? A guide to creating harmony in your home.* EverydayHealth.com. https://w ww.everydayhealth.com/photogallery/feng-shui-your-home.aspx

Raypole, C. (2020, September 27). *The beginner's guide to mirror gazing meditation.* Healthline. https://www.healthline.com/health/mental-he alth/mirror-gazing

Raypole, C. (2022, December 5). *Body scan meditation: Benefits and how to do it.* Healthline. https://www.healthline.com/health/body-scan-me ditation#benefits

Wein, H. (Ed.). (2012, January). NIH: news in health. *Newsin-health.Nih.Gov.* https://newsinhealth.nih.gov/sites/nihNIH/files/2 012/January/NIHNiHJan2012.pdf.

Printed in Great Britain
by Amazon

24493563R00020